READINGS ABOUT AMERICA

The SOUTHWEST Today

PICTURE CREDITS
Cover Tim Bean/Corbis; page 1 Dewitt Jones/Corbis; pages 2–3 B.S.P.I./Corbis; pages 4, 5 (top left), 11, 13, 14, 32 (bottom right) Photodisc; pages 4–5 (bottom), 7 (top and bottom), 9 (right) Michael Nichols/National Geographic Image Collection; page 5 (top right) Marie Read/Animals Animals/Earth Scenes; page 6 David Muench/Corbis; page 8 (top) Royalty-Free/Corbis; page 8 (bottom) Bill Hatcher/National Geographic Image Collection; page 9 (left) George H. H. Huey/Corbis; pages 10–11 Greg Probst/Corbis; page 13 Roger Garwood & Trish Ainslee/Corbis; pages 14–15 Buddy Mays/Corbis; page 16 Galen Rowell/Corbis; page 17 Layne Kennedy/Corbis; page 18 (top) John Cancalosi/National Geographic Image Collection; pages 18–19 Annie Griffiths Belt/National Geographic Image Collection; pages 20–21 Yann Arthus-Bertrand/Corbis; page 23 Strauss/Curtis/Corbis; page 24 William H. Campbell/National Geographic Image Collection; pages 24–25 Macduff Everton/Corbis; page 26 Sinclair Stammers/Science Photo Library/Photo Researchers; pages 27–29 Armando Adrian-Lopez/Photos courtesy of Scott Markman; pages 30 Gordon Gahan/National Geographic Image Collection; pages 30–31 Susan Kinast/Foodpix; page 32 (top) Dave G. Houser/Corbis; page 32 (middle left) Terry W. Eggers/Corbis; page 32 (middle right) National Cowboy & Western Heritage Museum, Oklahoma City, OK; page 32 (bottom left) Ray A. Valdez—Santa Fe Downtown Kiwanis Foundation.

back cover: Peppers
front cover: Grand Canyon overlook
page 1: Anasazi bowl
page 2–3: Saguaro cactus in Arizona

Produced through the worldwide resources of the National Geographic Society, John M. Fahey, Jr., President and Chief Executive Officer; Gilbert M. Grosvenor, Chairman of the Board; Nina D. Hoffman, Executive Vice President and President, Books and Education Publishing Group.

PREPARED BY NATIONAL GEOGRAPHIC SCHOOL PUBLISHING
Ericka Markman, Senior Vice President and President, Children's Books and Education Publishing Group; Steve Mico, Vice President, Editorial Director; Marianne Hiland, Executive Editor; Anita Schwartz, Project Editor; Jim Hiscott, Design Manager; Kristin Hanneman, Illustrations Manager; Diana Bourdrez, Picture Editor; Matt Wascavage, Manager of Publishing Services; Sean Philpotts, Production Manager.

MANUFACTURING AND QUALITY MANAGEMENT
Christopher A. Liedel, Chief Financial Officer; Phillip L. Schlosser, Director; Clifton M. Brown III, Manager.

PROGRAM DEVELOPMENT Gare Thompson Associates, Inc.

ART DIRECTION Dan Banks, Project Design Company

CONSULTANTS/REVIEWERS
Dr. Margit E. McGuire, School of Education, Seattle University, Seattle, Washington

BOOK DEVELOPMENT Nieman Inc.

BOOK DESIGN Three Communication Design, LLC

MAP DEVELOPMENT AND PRODUCTION Dave Stevenson

ARTWORK Tom Newsom

Published by the National Geographic Society
1145 17th Street, N.W.
Washington, D.C. 20036-4688

ISBN: 0-7922-4535-0
ISBN-13: 978-0-7922-4535-3

12
7

CONTENTS

THE SOUTHWEST

The Southwest is a region with natural wonders and strong cultural traditions. The Southwest had an exciting past, and it's a lot of fun out here today too!

To learn the answers to the following questions—and other interesting things about the Southwest—read on.

How did the "Lost Dutchman's Mine" get lost?

Find out on page 10.

ARIZONA

NEW MEXIC

N

W

E

S

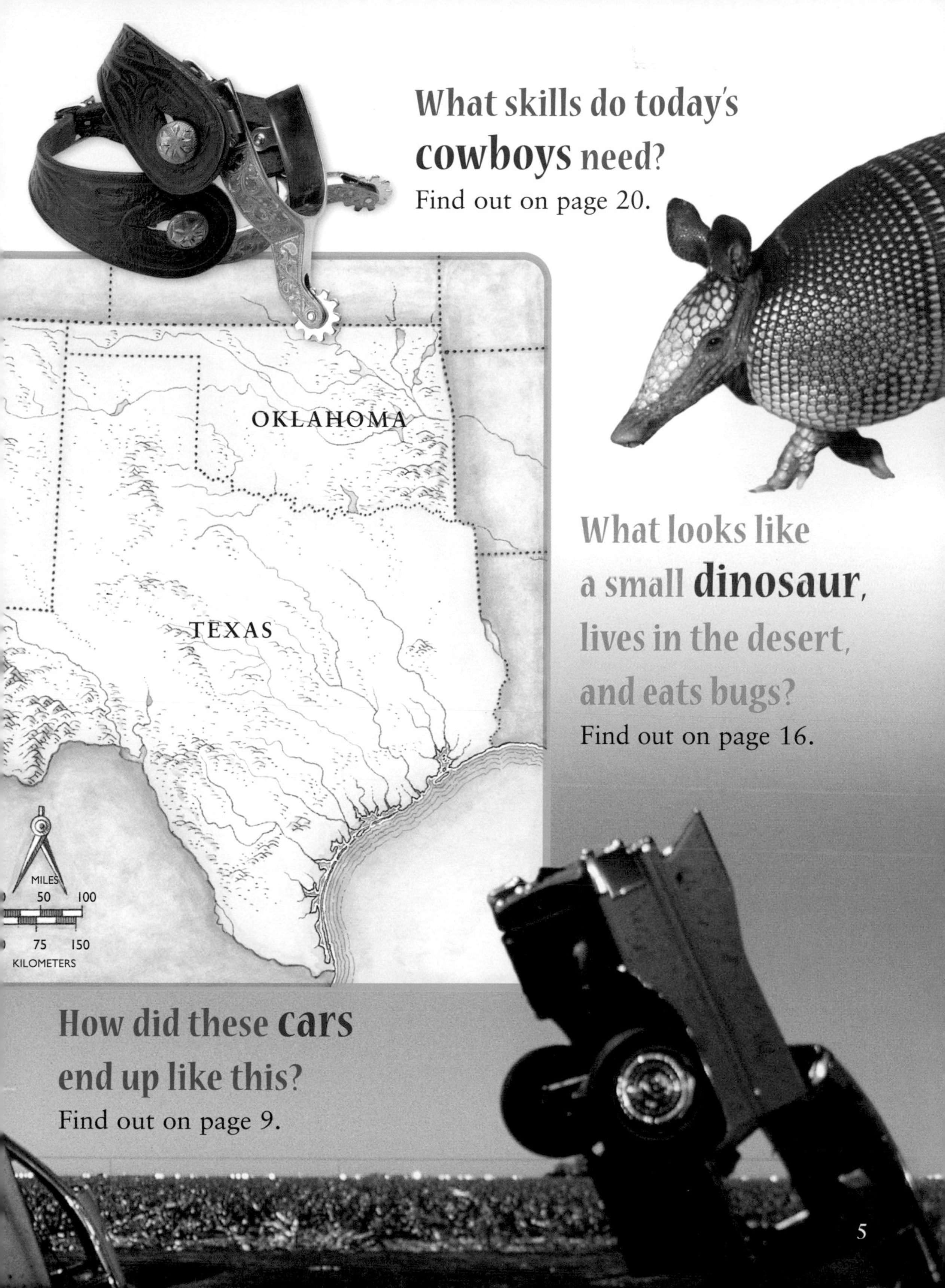

What skills do today's **cowboys** need?

Find out on page 20.

What looks like a small **dinosaur**, lives in the desert, and eats bugs?

Find out on page 16.

How did these **cars** end up like this?

Find out on page 9.

Touring the Southwest

By Lisa Moran

Here are two places in the Southwest you might enjoy visiting. The first is a vast underground world of caves that are millions of years old. The second place is where an ancient Native American people lived and then disappeared.

◀ Stalactites hang down over visitors' heads.

Carlsbad Caverns

Your first stop is Carlsbad Caverns in southwest New Mexico. Millions of years ago, a great sea covered this area. It's hard to imagine that this hot, dry spot was once underwater! Huge coral reefs formed in this ancient sea. When the water disappeared, the reefs remained as mountains. Rainwater dripped through the rock and carved out caves. They took millions of years to make!

You'll need to wear a jacket for your visit to Carlsbad Caverns. The temperature in the caves is only about 56 degrees. That may come as a surprise when it might be over 90 degrees in the desert outside!

Hundreds of feet underground, you'll see different types of strange rock formations. Stalactites (stuh–LAK–tites) hang from the cave ceiling like giant icicles. You might see the Ray of Light. That's a place where a huge beam of sunlight pours down through a hole in the cave ceiling.

Be sure not to miss the demonstrations of rope climbing. It's exciting watching people hanging from the cave ceiling on ropes! It takes a lot of special training and equipment to do it.

If you visit the Caverns between April and October you can see thousands of bats. They're Mexican free-tailed bats, and they live in the caves. The come out to feed on insects in the evening.

The Ray of Light pours into the main cavern.

Canyon De Chelly

Your next stop is Canyon de Chelly National Monument in northeast Arizona. Canyon de Chelly (shay) is the site of ruins of Native American villages built long ago. The ruins are at the base of steep red cliffs and in caves in the canyon walls. They were built by a Native American people known as the Anasazi. The Anasazi lived in the Southwest between about A.D. 100 and 1300. They were farmers. They also made baskets and pottery.

▲
Anasazi ruins at the bottom of a sandstone cliff

Spider Rock rising in the middle of Canyon de Chelly
▼

At first, the Anasazi lived mostly in pithouses. They simply dug big holes in the ground and covered them with branches and mud. Later, they started building houses above the ground. These houses were built of stone or mud brick. Some of these houses were as big as apartment buildings!

Around 1300, the Anasazi seem to have disappeared. Scientists aren't sure what happened to them. They know there were droughts in the years before the Anasazi disappeared. Without rain, the Anasazi crops would have died. Another theory is that the Anasazi were driven away by their enemies. They also could have merged with other Native American peoples, such as the Hopi or the Navajo. No one knows for certain—it's a mystery.

ROADSIDE **America**

Cadillac Ranch

Down the road from Amarillo, Texas, is a place called Cadillac Ranch. What do you think they raise there? Cattle? Wrong! It's where some artists made a weird sculpture by sticking 10 old cars into the ground. You're allowed to put graffiti on the cars! People from all over the world have written things in lots of different languages. Be sure to bring some spray paint!

◀ Anasazi pottery

Folklore

The Legend of the Lost Dutchman's Mine

By Gare Thompson

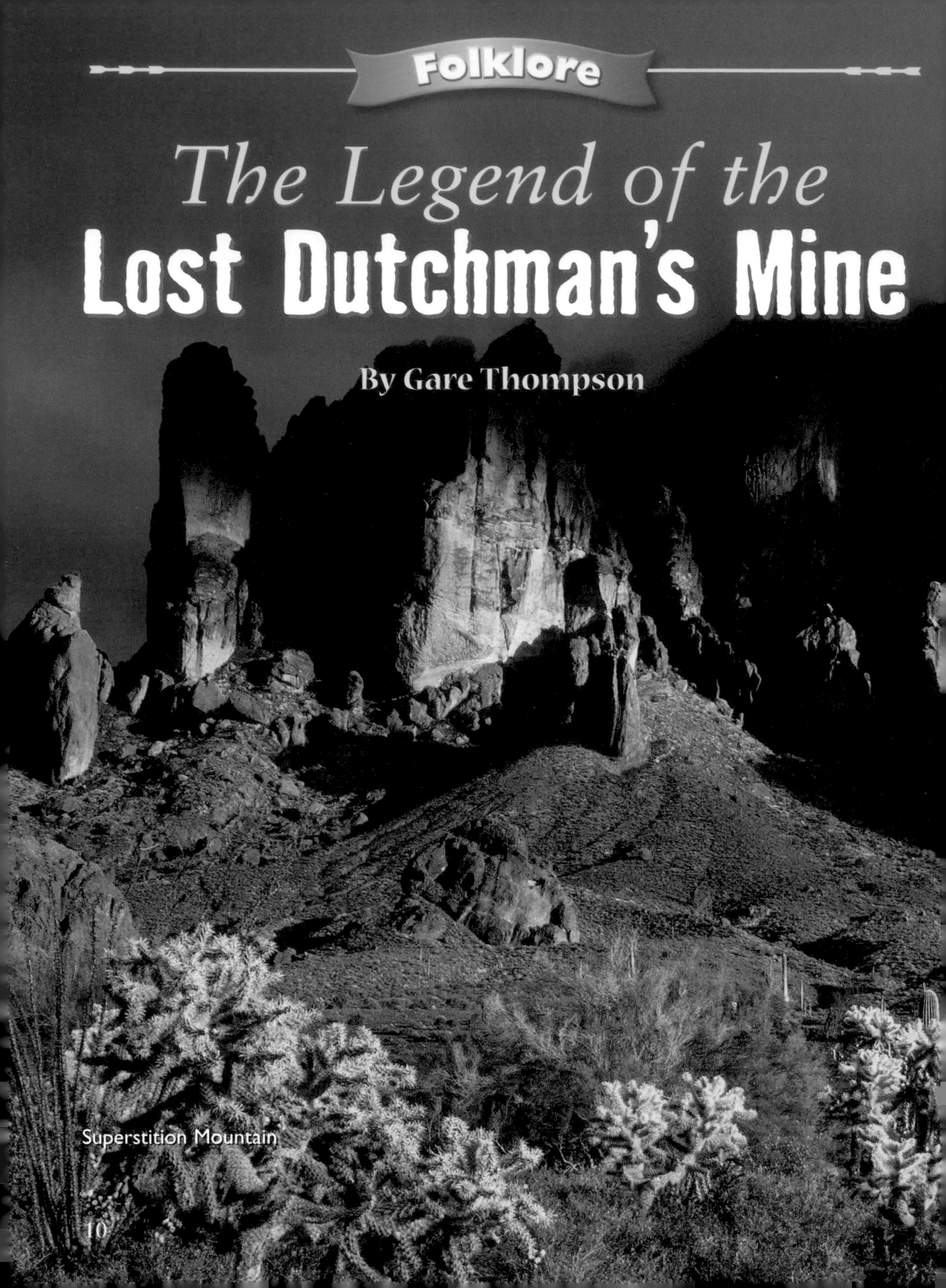

Superstition Mountain

Gold lay everywhere, according to the stories. Gold nuggets as big as hens' eggs covered the ground. Veins of gold snaked through the rocks. Chips of gold gleamed in the hot sand. There was so much gold that the glitter hurt your eyes.

Everyone wanted the gold, but fear stopped most people from searching for it. The stories said that a Mexican named Peralta had first found the gold, but Apaches killed most of his 600 men. The Mexicans had disturbed the Apaches' sacred mountain.

People called this spot in southern Arizona "Superstition Mountain." They told stories of hidden wealth and sudden death. Somewhere on Superstition Mountain a fortune in gold was still waiting—for someone daring enough to find it.

In the 1860s, Jacob Waltz moved to Arizona from Germany. A shabby miner, Waltz looked older than his 50 years. He had lived a hard life, but once Waltz heard the stories he had a dream. He didn't care about the dangers. He would find the gold!

One night, Waltz heard someone talk about Peralta. He listened carefully, his dark eyes glittering. "I'll find that mine," he said.

Suddenly, Waltz dropped out of sight. All winter, no one saw him. Cold winds blew from Superstition Mountain. People began to wonder if Waltz had died out there. Then, just as suddenly, he was back. That wasn't all. Waltz looked like he had struck it rich!

He wore new wool trousers. He had on a bright, cotton shirt. Where were his old, shabby clothes? How had he earned the money for his new duds? Waltz never said. He kept quiet. When people asked him if he had found the gold, Waltz just shrugged.

One day Waltz walked into the local store. He bought a new blanket, saddle, and stove. People stared. Then Waltz bought a wagonload of food. He paid with gold nuggets. People's jaws dropped as the stunned clerk counted the nuggets. No one had seen that much gold in a long time. No one dared say anything to Waltz.

People's jaws dropped as the stunned clerk counted the nuggets.

Waltz had found the mine, but now he had a problem. He couldn't get all the gold out by himself. So, he took only the nuggets and small pieces that he could carry. He hid as much gold in different places as he could. Also, Waltz didn't know anyone he could trust. He thought that he would be able to get the gold out later. What should he do about the mine? Waltz decided to hide it.

First, he rolled boulders into the opening. The boulders looked like part of the mountain. Then Waltz covered the boulders with dirt and planted a few bushes there. He drew a detailed map of the spot. Then he returned home. Waltz felt that his mine was safely hidden. He had hidden gold around the mountain, but nowhere near the mine. Someone might find this gold, but they would not find his mine.

Waltz lived quietly in a small cabin for the next few years. People knew where his cabin was. They spied on him. No one saw him go near a mine. About once a year, Waltz would disappear.

Waltz felt that his mine was safely hidden.

He seemed to vanish in the middle of the night. No one spotted him leaving. No one knew where he went. But each time he returned with chunks of shiny gold.

Waltz wanted to return to his mine one day. He knew he couldn't keep it hidden forever. Then the unexpected happened. Waltz was caught in a flash flood during a storm. He was chilled and became ill. On October 25, 1891, Waltz died.

Soon, people began to talk about "the Lost Dutchman's Mine." Over time, thousands of people have hunted for this mine. They have lost their lives and fortunes looking for it. Some people wonder if it ever really existed. Dozens of maps have surfaced, each claiming to be the one that Waltz made. None has led anyone to the mine.

Today, Superstition Mountain is part of Lost Dutchman State Park, near Phoenix, Arizona. Perhaps you should visit Superstition Mountain. Maybe you'll find the Lost Dutchman's Mine!

Tourists riding a trail at Lost Dutchman State Park

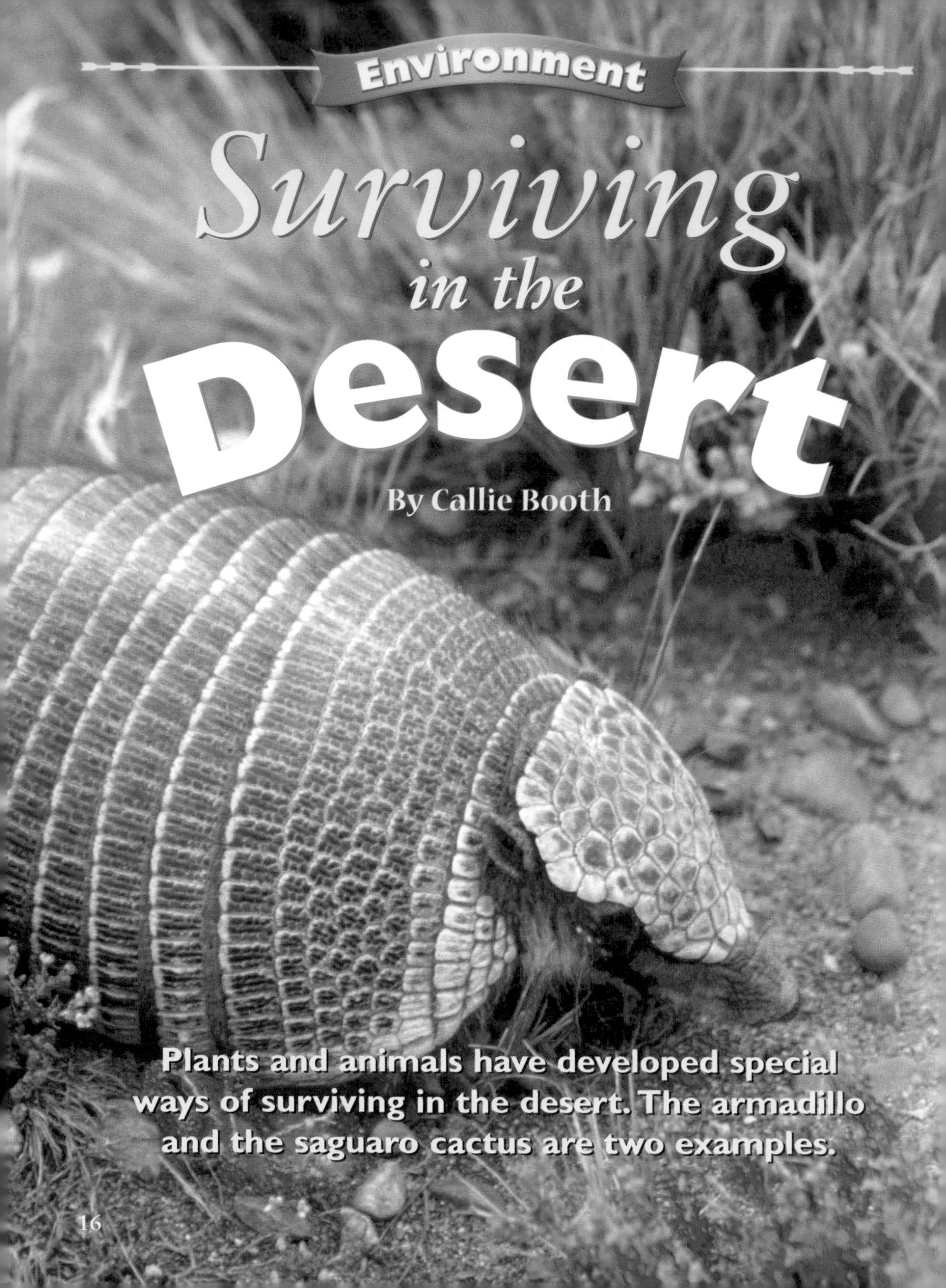

Environment

Surviving in the Desert

By Callie Booth

Plants and animals have developed special ways of surviving in the desert. The armadillo and the saguaro cactus are two examples.

Nights in Armor

The sun sets on a sweltering summer day in western Texas. A twisted tree looms above a burrow. A small head pokes out. This armadillo is an odd-looking animal. Its ears stick up above a long, narrow head covered in weird, scaly skin. The animal's tiny eyes seem half-closed. It first sniffs the air and then comes the rest of the way out of its burrow.

The armadillo moves away from the tree. Night darkens the desert, but that doesn't stop this insect-eater. The armadillo is hunting bugs. It hopes to find anthills, termite mounds, and stray scorpions and spiders. Armadillos have pretty bad eyesight—even during the day. They depend on their keen sense of smell to find food. Suddenly, the armadillo stops. Its nose knows that smell! In a flash, its powerful clawed feet tear into a fire ants' nest. A sticky tongue shoots out of its long snout. It happily licks up the stinging ants.

The next stop on the armadillo's nighttime hunt is a creek. Fire ants sure cause a powerful thirst! The armadillo doesn't stop at the creek's edge. It walks into the water and disappears.

Next, we see the armadillo crawling onto the bank on the creek's far side. It just strolled across the creek bottom. After a short mud bath, the armadillo returns to the hunt. It will search over several acres of land tonight. At sunrise, the armadillo will return to its burrow.

▲
Cactus in bloom in western Texas

Days Without Rain

What southwestern desert plant can grow taller than a house? This plant lives twice as long as a person. It weighs as much as a truck. And it has its own national park named after it. It's the giant saguaro (suh–WAR–oh) cactus! These massive plants are the biggest cacti in the United States. Some live for two centuries.

Saguaros live in the Sonoran Desert of Arizona. The giant cactus is food for many desert animals. Their sweet fruit is a favorite treat of birds, squirrels, ants, and the javelina (hah–vuh–LEE–nuh), a wild pig. Bats, bees, and moths sip the nectar of its flowers. The giant cactus is also home for many desert animals. More than a dozen kinds of birds, including owls and woodpeckers, nest in or on the giant plant.

Summer days in the desert are often over 100 degrees. Months go by between rainstorms. So, how does this old giant survive? It doesn't waste water! Saguaros have no leaves, because leaves draw out water. A waxy outer skin seals in a saguaro's water.

Saguaros soak up and store a lot of rainwater. The roots of a saguaro form a wide web that stretches out as far as the giant cactus is tall. Those roots can soak up hundreds of gallons of water from a single downpour. The saguaro's accordion-like trunk unfolds as it swells to store the extra water. This desert giant can survive an entire year on one good rainfall.

◀ A hawk and its baby make a home for themselves on the giant cactus.

The **giant cactus** *is home for many desert animals.*

Technology and Change

CHANGING TIMES on the Ranch

By Liz West

A ranch today combines the best of modern technology with the romance of the Old West. Modern ranchers have the skills that made the American cowboy famous. They can ride and rope with the best of them. However, they also have tools and knowledge that were unknown in the past.

The ranching way of life really began almost 150 years ago. In the years after the Civil War, more beef was needed to feed the people in America's growing cities. There were millions of cattle in Texas. The problem was how to get them to the towns along the railroad lines. From there, the cattle would be shipped east to meatpacking plants. These towns were hundreds of miles from Texas. The solution was the cattle drive.

A cattle drive could last for several months. The herd moved about 15 miles a day. During this time, cowboys lived outdoors and worked 18 hours a day, 7 days a week. They worked in heat and dust, in wind and rain. At night, they slept in bedrolls under the open sky. Around 35,000 cowboys found work on ranches. Many were freed slaves, Native Americans, or Mexicans. Most were young and strong. A cowboy's life was hard.

Cowboys may also fly helicopters or ride snowmobiles.

Old Time Cowboy Gear

A cowboy's clothing and gear weren't just part of a colorful costume. Everything had a purpose.

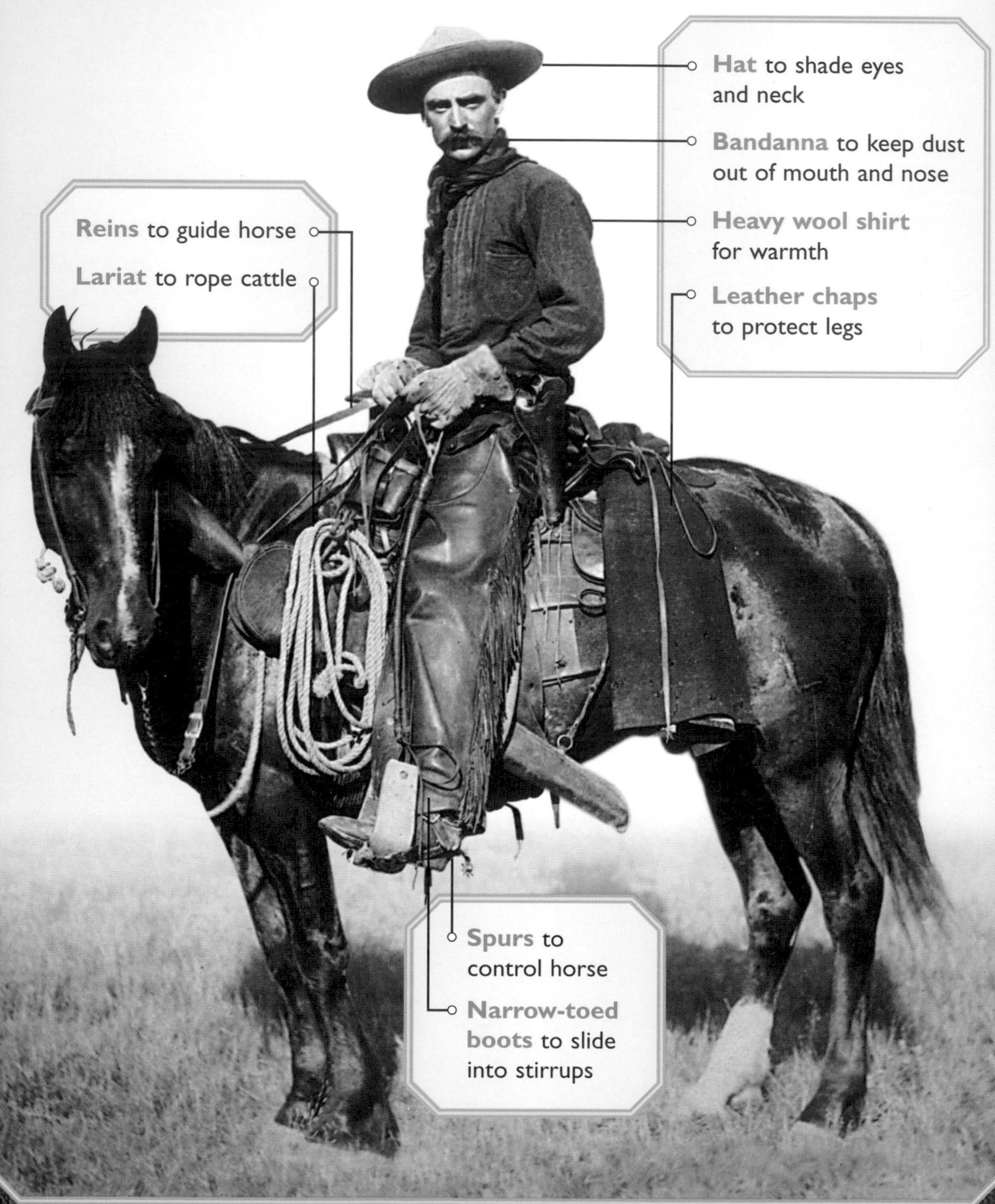

The Modern Ranch

Things have changed a lot on the ranch from the days of the cattle drives. Even the cattle have changed! In the old days, they were Texas longhorns, tough animals that could survive the harsh conditions of a long drive. New breeds of cattle met the need for more tender beef, but breeding these cattle was costly. Ranchers saw them as big investments.

Today, ranches reflect these changes. Now cattle are raised on fenced ranches. Electronic tags track their movements. Modern ranchers need to know about cattle breeding, cattle health, and markets. They must know which feedlots have grass and grains that are best for cattle.

Cowboys as well as owners have new skills. Most workers double as mechanics, carpenters, and farmers. They fix trailers, dig postholes, put up fences, and grease windmills. They make hay, use computers, and drive trucks. Although horses are still vital to round-ups, cowboys may also fly helicopters or ride snowmobiles.

They no longer sleep under the stars. Now they sleep in cabins or trailers. But they still get up before dawn and work all day. Their way of life has changed, but it hasn't disappeared.

Today's cowboys use cell phones.

Get Ready to Rock

It is Saturday. Kids across the Southwest are rolling out of their beds before dawn.

They are not yet awake, but they have a lot to do. They stuff backpacks with rock hammers and hardhats, gloves and goggles, and brushes and bubble wrap. They eat a good breakfast. Then they pull on old jeans and sturdy boots. These rock hounds are getting ready—to get dirty.

Just what is a rock hound? It's someone who likes to collect rocks. Rock hounding is a hobby.

▲ Rock hounds coming home with buckets loaded with rocks

By Adam McClellam

People all over the world enjoy it—both young and old. Rock hounds get to enjoy the outdoors with friends and family. Rock hounding is also a great way to learn about geology.

Geology is the science that studies how Earth began, how it changes, and what it is made of. Rocks can tell a lot about Earth's history.

Rock hounding is a hobby that is popular in the Southwest. Why? Dry scrub or desert covers much of the Southwest. So, lots of rocks can be spotted right on the surface. You don't have to dig! The rocks are out in the open. Trees, plants, and soil don't cover or hide them. This makes the Southwest perfect for rock hounding.

Rock hounds hunt for many different kinds of rocks. They can find many kinds easily. A favorite kind is a **fossil**. Fossils are rocks that contain traces of plants and animals that lived long ago. We're not talking about huge dinosaur bones. Smaller fossils of ancient sea creatures are very common. You find them in ditches, road cuts, and desert washes. Rock hounds explore old mines and other sites too. They look for **crystals**, or transparent rocks, such as **quartz**. These glassy rocks are fun to find.

Rock Hounds at Home

The work doesn't stop when rock hounds get home. Many young rock hounds work on their personal rock collections. They clean, polish, sort, and label their finds. Some people belong to rock hound clubs. The clubs help local museums build their collections. They show the rocks and minerals to the public.

Rock hounds also like to meet at rock and gem shows. Here, collectors show off what they've found. They buy, sell, and swap rocks, fossils, and crystals of all sorts. And they talk about the best places to go rock hounding. Many say it's the Southwest!

Here are some things every rock hound needs:

rock hammer with sheath
A rock hammer is a solid piece of steel, so the head won't break off. If you keep it in a sheath you'll be less likely to lose it.

specimen containers
Newspaper, bubble wrap, garbage bags, egg cartons, cardboard boxes, or plastic buckets are all strong enough to hold what you find.

safety goggles!!!
You need to protect your eyes from splinters.

other protective stuff
You never know when a hard-hat, gloves, sunscreen, or first aid kit will come in handy.

water and snacks
It's a desert out there!

Words for You

crystal a transparent rock

fossil a rock that contains traces of plants and animals that lived long ago

geology the science that studies how Earth began, how it changes, and what it is made of

quartz a type of crystal

Close-up of quartz crystal ▶

The Magician's Grandson

Armando Lopez of New Mexico is an artist. He always wanted to be one. His grandfather was a local craftsman who made baskets, toys, and **ceramics.** "I thought he was a magician," Armando says. "He could make everything." Armando decided to take up his grandfather's craft.

His parents encouraged him. "When I was little and made drawings, my family always said, 'Draw another one.' Soon I thought of myself as an artist." Armando kept drawing.

Sculpture of San Isidro, the patron saint of farmers

By Chloe Thompson

Armando's Art

Armando loves Mexican **folk art**. Folk art is the traditional art made by untrained artists. Mexican folk art uses simple, natural materials, such as clay and cornhusks. Armando starts with natural materials, such as grasses and twigs. He also uses pearls, gold, and **egg tempera**. This is a kind of paint in which the color is mixed with egg yolk. He makes this paint himself.

When Armando makes human figures, he starts with the face. "That gives me ideas for what I want to portray with the hands and body," he says. Then he goes on to make the neck and body. Finally, he makes the hands and legs.

Armando repeats certain themes. He makes many saints and angels, like those shown here. Today, many people admire Armando's work, the same way that he first admired the work of his grandfather. Armando is now a magician too.

ceramics objects made from clay, hardened in an oven

egg tempera a kind of paint in which the color is mixed with egg yolk

folk art traditional art made by artists who are untrained

The story of the angel who helped the boy Tobias comes from the Bible.

Lopez's Noah's Ark is made from many different pieces.

Culture and Diversity

Hot, Hott

By James Santos

Are you tough enough to taste something called "Sally's Screaming Scorcher" or "Frank's Five-Alarmer"? You could find out in Texas. Texas hosts some of this country's biggest and hottest chili cook-offs.

Under colorful tents, which offer shelter from the hot sun, contestants work all day to cook up large pots of bubbling chili. Chili is a type of stew. True Texas chili contains just meat and spices. It has no beans. In other places, chili is made with beans. Sometimes, it's even meatless.

Huge chili cook-offs are part carnival and part contest. Bands play, vendors sell food, and people dress up like Mr. and Mrs. Chili Pepper. Cooks often wear costumes or aprons labeled "Hot Stuff" and "Kiss the Cook."

Each cook must make several gallons of chili. The chili has to be cooked that day, starting from scratch. Contest chili isn't like the chili most people eat at home. It's usually much hotter. The secret of this heat lies in the chili peppers.

▲ Tasting at the cook-off

, Hottest!

Hot Enough for You?

Although chilies use many spices, most stews contain chili peppers. These colorful vegetables are used throughout the world. A chili pepper can be white, red, green, yellow, orange, even purple or black. The shapes differ as well. Some peppers are almost round, while others are skinny and pointed.

Chili peppers can be mild or hot. In general, small peppers are hotter than large ones. The tiny habañeros are the hottest peppers in the world. These can blister skin. The peppers used at cook-offs are usually very hot.

A cook-off judge who likes a chili will often say, "Great kick!" However, to make sure the chili doesn't carry too much of a wallop, many cook-offs have a safety rule. Cooks have to taste their chili before feeding it to a judge.

What's Hot! What's Not!

A chili's heat comes from a chemical in the pepper. A chemist invented a way to measure this heat. His name was Wilbur Scoville. Today, a chili's heat is shown in Scoville units.

Habañero Pepper
300,000 Scoville units

Cayenne Pepper
30,000 Scoville units

Jalapeño Pepper
5,000 Scoville units

Sweet Bell Pepper
0 Scoville units

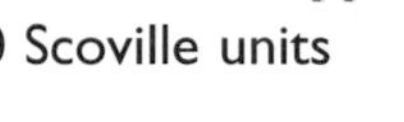

Insider's Guide

Here are a few more special places that make the Southwest interesting and fun.

Want to learn more about the desert? Then visit the **Arizona-Sonoran Desert Museum** near Tucson, Arizona. It's a natural history museum, zoo, and garden—all in one place. You can learn about more than 300 kinds of animals and 1,200 kinds of plants. What's even better, you see them alive in their natural desert environment.

Feel like returning to the Old West? You might want to visit the **National Cowboy and Western Heritage Museum** in Oklahoma City, Oklahoma. You can wander around Prosperity Junction, a replica of an Old West cattle town.

Just for fun, you might join the crowds at the **annual fiesta in Santa Fe, New Mexico.** Held each September for almost 200 years, the fiesta begins with the burning of Zozobra. Zozobra, or "Old Man Gloom," is a 50-foot high papier-mâché figure that represents everyone's troubles during the past year.